Brain Teasers with Coding for Data Scientist

VIRAG R SHAH

BRAIN TEASERS WITH CODING FOR DATA SCIENTIST

By

Virag R Shah

November 2020

Publish by: Self-Published
Virag R Shah

India

For additional information, contact the author.

Virag R. Shah: viragbook@gmail.com
https://byte-man.com

DISCLAIMER

Every effort has been made to avoid errors or omissions in the publication. In spite of this, some errors might have crept in. The publisher or author shall not be responsible for the same. Any mistake, error or discrepancy noted may be brought to our notice which shall be taken care of in the next edition. It is notified that neither the publisher nor the author will be responsible for any damage or loss of action of any one, of any kind, in any manner, therefore.

ACKNOWLEDGMENTS

First of all, I want to thank you for choosing this book, 'Brain Teasers with Coding for Data Scientist'. I sincerely hope you will enjoy the brain teasers in this book.

The brain teasers are chosen from a collection of problems that I have encountered over the years in interviews, books, websites and blogs. They are represented in a generalized form in this book.

CONTENTS

INTRODUCTION

Brain teasers, kind of puzzles built for lateral thinking, can help to improve cognitive skills. Lateral thinking is a way of solving problems using an indirect and creative approach via reasoning that is not immediately obvious. It involves ideas that may not be obtainable using only traditional step-by-step logic.

Traditionally during software engineering or analytics positions hiring, some companies may ask brain teaser(s) to test how a candidate thinks and approaches a new problem when faced with one. Data Science started with statistics has evolved to include the concepts of software engineering and so does its hiring practices. Whether you are trying to improve your coding skills or preparing for a data science interview, you should at least try on them to test your critical thinking and logic. In data science, statistics is a great supplement to the traditional coding brain teasers.

In this book, you will find interesting brain teasers that are suitable for data scientists as well as software engineers. This is a unique book where solutions are given with coding. So, get ready and jump into the world of fascinating and exciting brain teasers.

PYTHON LANGUAGE

Python is the most widely used data science programming language in the world today. It is very easy-to-learn programming language even for beginners and newcomers because of its not complicated simplified syntax which gives more emphasis on natural language. The simplicity of Python and its easily human-readable syntax are two prime reasons why the language is so popular among non-programmers or developers. I have provided the coding solutions of brain teasers in python.

If you haven't installed Python on your desktop or laptop and don't know how to install it then search online or visit: https://byte-man.com/how-to-install-python/ and for basic introduction of Python: https://byte-man.com/basic-introduction-to-python/ For Python installation and basic learning, various resources, tutorials and videos are easily available on the internet.

If you don't want to install Python on your machine, you can still learn or code the program by using online compiler like onlinegdb.com, programiz.com or any other but it should be Python 3 compiler for the solutions provided in this book. (Kindly Note: Python 3 or higher version is strongly recommended for any new development or learning.)

Brain Teasers with Coding for Data Scientist

1 HELLO WORLD

Let's start with basic coding. Python and R are the most widely used programming languages among others (for example, Java, Scala, Matlab) for data science.

Python code snippet is given below:

```
if <condition>:
   print("Hello")
else:
   print("World")
```

What's the <condition> so that the code snippet prints "Hello World"?

2 BASIC CODING

Print 'I am 10th' in every computer language you know.

3 N ANTS

Imagine there are N ants in N different corners of an equilateral polygon, and each ant randomly picks a direction and starts traversing the edge of the polygon. What's the probability that none of the ants collide? (Provided condition: N>2)

Write a code.

4 DEATH RAT

You have X wine bottles, one of which is poisoned. You want to determine which bottle is poisoned by feeding the wine to the rats. The poisoned wine takes Z hour to work. How many rats are necessary to find the poisoned bottle in Y hour? (Provided condition: Y is multiple of Z.)

Write a code.

5 BIRTHDAY MATCH

There are X students in the class. What is the possibility that at least 2 students share the same day of birth? (Provided condition: No student is born in a leap year.)

Write a code.

6 FAIR COIN

Make a fair (unbiased) coin from an unfair (biased) coin.

Write a code.

7 N COINS

You have an N coins laying flat on a table, each with a head side and a tail side. M of them are heads up, rest are tails up. You can't feel, see or in any other way find out which M are heads up. Your goal: split the coins into two piles in such a way that there are the same numbers of heads-up coins in each pile.

Write a code.

8 N BAGS

You have N bags full of coins. In each bag are infinite coins. But one bag is full of forgeries, and you can't remember which one. But you do know that genuine coins weigh 1 gram, but forgeries weigh 1.1 grams. You have to identify that bag in minimum readings. You are provided with a digital weighing machine.

Write a code.

9 RAIN IN THE CITY

You are about to get on a plane to Mumbai, you want to know whether you have to bring an umbrella or not. You call N of your random friends and ask each one of them if it's raining. The probability that your any friend is telling the truth is 2/3 and the probability that (s)he is playing a prank on you by lying is 1/3. If all N of them tell that it is raining, then what is the probability that it is actually raining in Mumbai.

Write a code.

10 N PRISONERS & N BOXES

The director of a prison offers N death row prisoners, who are numbered from 1 to N, a last chance. A room contains a cupboard with N boxes. The director randomly puts one prisoner's number in each closed boxes. The prisoners enter the room, one after another. Each prisoner may open and look into N/2 boxes in any order. The boxes are closed again afterwards. If, during this search, every prisoner finds his number in one of the boxes, all prisoners are pardoned. If just one prisoner does not find his number, all prisoners die. Before the first prisoner enters the room, the prisoners may discuss strategy — but may not communicate once the first prisoner enters to look in the boxes. What is the prisoners' best strategy?

Write a code.

11 BALLS ON A PLANE

How many numbers of balls with radius 'r' can fit in an airplane of length L and interior radius R?

Write a code.

12 4 N

You are given any number. Let's assume N is given. Find an equation that use only that number 4 times in such a way that you will get an output number which consists of two numbers N+1 and N. (Provided condition: N>0)

Write a code.

13 N-DISTANCES

There are 4 cities placed on each corner of a square. Distance from one city to other adjacent is N km. You need to build a road connecting those cities in a least cost.

Write a code.

14 THE PE NTAGON

You have to create the connecting passage between each corner of an equilateral Pentagon building. However you don't know the length of the side of the building? What should be your total minimum construction cost if the minimum construction cost per meter is R bucks?

Write a code.

15 N COLORS CHAMELEONS

A remote jungle has N colors of chameleons. They wonder and meet in pairs. When two chameleons of different colors meet, they both change to the third color. Given initial amounts of the chameleons of each color are C_1, C_2, ... and C_N, may this happen that, after a while, all of them acquire the same color?

Write a code.

Solutions

1 HELLO WORLD SOLUTION

The below program prints "Hello World"

```
if print("Hello", end =" "):
    print("Hello")
else:
    print("World")
```

Explanation:

Here, <condition> = print("Hello", end =" ")

In Python : print() function doesn't return anything (so it's None).

By default Python's print() function ends with a newline. You can end a print statement with any character/string using this parameter. Let's see

```
# default end parameter '\n'
print("Hello")
print("World")
-- Output is --
Hello
World
```

```
# Now change end parameter value
# ends the output with a <space>
print("Hello " , end = ' ')
print("World" , end = ' ')
-- Output is --
Hello World
```

Extra: what is the output of below code?

```
print(print())
print("***")
print(print("Hello World"))
print("***")
print(print(print("Hello World")))
```

Output you will get is shown below:
```
None

***

Hello World

None

***

Hello World

None

None
```

2 BASIC CODING SOLUTION

Code is provided in 10 popular programming languages.
1. C
2. Python
3. Java
4. C++
5. C#
6. Visual Basic
7. JavaScript
8. PHP
9. R
10. SQL

1. C

```c
#include <stdio.h>

int main() {
    printf("I am 10th");
    return 0;
}
```

2. Python

```python
print("I am 10th")
```

3. Java

```java
public class HelloWorld{

    public static void main(String []args){
        System.out.println("I am 10th");
    }

}
```

4. C++

```cpp
#include <iostream>


int main()
{
    printf("I am 10th");
    return 0;
}
```

5. C#

```csharp
using System.IO;
using System;

class Program
{
    static void Main()
    {
        Console.WriteLine("I am 10th");
    }
}
```

6. Visual Basic

```vb
Module VBModule
    Sub Main()
        Console.WriteLine("I am 10th")
    End Sub
End Module
```

7. JavaScript

```html
<!DOCTYPE html>
<html>
<body>
<p id="tenth"></p>
```

```
<script>
document.getElementById("tenth").innerHTML = "I
am 10th"
</script>

</body>
</html>
```

8. PHP

```
<?php print("I am 10th"); ?>
```

9. R

```
print("I am 10th")
```

10. SQL

```
BEGIN TRANSACTION;
CREATE TABLE FORPRINT(Id integer
PRIMARY KEY);
COMMIT;

SELECT 'I am 1'||count(*)||'th' FROM
FORPRINT where 1=2;
```

3 N ANTS SOLUTION

There are only two possibilities in which collision can be occurred.

- All ants move in counterclockwise direction.
- All ants move in anti-counterclockwise direction.

Since every ant has two choices (pick either of two edges going through the corner on which ant is initially sitting). So for N ants there are total 2^N possibilities.

Probability that none of the ants collide $= (2^N - 2)/ 2^N$

$$= (2^{N-1} - 1)/ 2^{N-1}$$

```
import math
# Non Collide Probability for N ANTS

# N Number of Ants & N > 2
N = 3

# P Probability
P = (math.pow(2,N-1)-1)/math.pow(2,N-1)

print('Probability that none of', N,
'ants collide:', P)
```

Output:
Probability that none of 3 ants collide: 0.75

If you set N = 4 then output:
Probability that none of 4 ants collide: 0.875

If you set N = 10 then output:
Probability that none of 10 ants collide: 0.998046875

4 DEATH RAT SOLUTION

General Formula:

$$\mathbf{Log}_{\frac{Y+1}{Z}}(\mathbf{X})$$

:

Where X = Number of wine bottles
Z = Hours for poison to effect
Y = Hours to find a poisoned bottle

```
import math

#X wine bottles
X=1000
#Z hour time after which the poison
works
Z=24
#Y hour time to find the poisoned
bottle
Y=48

T = Y/Z

print ("Number of rats required to find
the poisoned bottle: ", end="")
print (math.ceil(math.log(X,T+1)))
```

Output:
Number of rats required to find the poisoned bottle: 7

Now if X=1000
Z=1
Y=1

Then output:
Number of rats required to find the poisoned bottle: 10

Now if X=240
Z=24
Y=48

Then output:
Number of rats required to find the poisoned bottle: 5

5 BIRTHDAY MATCH SOLUTION

General Formula:

$$1 - \frac{365!}{(365-N)! * 365^N}$$

Where N = Number of Students in a Class

```
# N Number of Students in Class
N = 35

mul1 = 1
for x in range(365-N+1,366):
    mul1 = mul1 * x


base = 365
exponent = N
mul2 = pow(base, exponent)
print('Probability of any two share
same birthday:',1-(mul1/mul2))
```

If N=35 then output:
Probability of any two share same birthday:
0.8143832388747152

If N=23 then output:
Probability of any two share same birthday:

0.5072972343239854

If N=40 then output:
Probability of any two share same birthday:
0.891231809817949

6 FAIR COIN SOLUTION

John von Neumann described the procedure like this:
1. Toss the coin twice.
2. If the outcome of both coins is the same (HH or TT), start over and disregard the current toss.
3. If the outcome of both coins is different (HT or TH), take the first coin as the result and forget the second.

```
from random import randint

# Biased function that returns Heads
with 60% probability and
# Tails with 40% probability
def toss_biased():

    # generate random number between 1-
100, both inclusive
    r = randint(1, 100)

    # return T if we got number between
[1-40], else return T
    return T if (r < 41) else H

def toss_unbiased():
  # difference = 0 in case of HH or TT
toss again
  # difference > 0 in case of HT return
H
  # difference < 0 in case of TH return
T
```

```
    difference = toss_biased() -
toss_biased()
    if difference > 0:
      return H
    if difference < 0:
      return T
    return toss_unbiased()


# Generate Fair Results from a Biased
Coin
if __name__ == '__main__':

    # Head
    H = 1
    # Tail
    T = 0

    head_count = tail_count = 0

    for i in range(10000):
        val = toss_unbiased()

        if val == 1:
            head_count += 1
        else:
            tail_count += 1

    print("HEADS% ~", head_count / 100,
"%")      # ~50%
    print("TAILS% ~", tail_count / 100,
"%")      # ~50%
```

Output:
HEADS% ~ 50.21 %
TAILS% ~ 49.79 %

Again run then output:
HEADS% ~ 49.95 %
TAILS% ~ 50.05 %

7 N COINS SOLUTION

1.) If there are M heads-up coins in N coins then pick randomly M coins from the given N coins and create two piles. (M coins, (N-M) coins)

2.) Flip all coins from a pile of M coins. You're done. You have successfully created two piles so that there are the same numbers of heads-up coins in each pile.

```
from random import randint
import array as arr


# Random function that returns N Coins
with M Heads
def random_coins():

    # generate random number either 1
or 0
    r = randint(0, 1)

    # return Head if we got number 1,
else return T
    return H if (r == 1) else T

# Generate Two Piles with Same Number
of Heads-up Coins
if __name__ == '__main__':

    # Head
    H = 1
    # Tail
```

```
T = 0

head_count = tail_count = 0

#Number of coins, let's take 100
N = 100
coins = []

for i in range(N):
    val = random_coins()
    if val == 1:
        head_count += 1
        coins.append(1)
    else:
        tail_count += 1
        coins.append(0)

print('Randomly Generated Coins')
print(coins)
print('In single pile of', N,
'coins:', head_count, 'are Heads and ',
tail_count, ' are Tails')
print('***Solution for splitting
the coins into two piles***')

pile1_coins = coins[0:head_count]
print('Size of 1st piles coins:',
len(pile1_coins))
print('1st piles coins:',
pile1_coins)
pile2_coins =
coins[len(pile1_coins):N]
```

```python
    print('Size of 2nd piles coins:',
len(pile2_coins))
    print('2nd piles coins:',
pile2_coins)

    pile1_coins_head = pile2_coins_head
= 0

    print('flip all coins of 1st pile')
    for g in range(len(pile1_coins)):
        if pile1_coins[g] == 1:
            pile1_coins[g] = 0
        else:
            pile1_coins[g] = 1

    print('1st piles coins after a
flip:', pile1_coins)

    for j in range(len(pile1_coins)):
        if pile1_coins[j] == 1:
            pile1_coins_head += 1

    for k in range(len(pile2_coins)):
        if pile2_coins[k] == 1:
            pile2_coins_head += 1

    print('Number of coins with head in
1st pile:', pile1_coins_head)

    print('Number of coins with head in
2nd pile:', pile2_coins_head)
```

Output:

Randomly Generated Coins
[0, 1, 1, 0, 0, 0, 1, 1, 0, 0, 0, 0, 0, 1, 1, 1, 1, 0, 0, 1, 0, 0, 0,
0, 0, 0, 0, 0, 0, 0, 1, 0, 1, 1, 1, 0, 1, 1, 0, 0, 1, 0, 0, 0, 1, 0, 1,
1, 0, 1, 0, 1, 0, 1, 1, 1, 0, 0, 1, 0, 1, 0, 1, 0, 1, 0, 0, 1, 1, 1, 1,
1, 1, 1, 0, 0, 0, 1, 0, 1, 1, 1, 0, 1, 1, 0, 1, 0, 1, 1, 1, 1, 0, 0, 0,
0, 0, 0, 0, 1]

In single pile of 100 coins: 47 are Heads and 53 are Tails

Solution for splitting the coins into two piles
Size of 1st piles coins: 47
1st piles coins: [0, 1, 1, 0, 0, 0, 1, 1, 0, 0, 0, 0, 0, 1, 1, 1,
1, 0, 0, 1, 0, 0, 0, 0, 0, 0, 0, 0, 0, 0, 1, 0, 1, 1, 1, 0, 1, 1, 0, 0,
1, 0, 0, 0, 1, 0, 1]

Size of 2nd piles coins: 53
2nd piles coins: [1, 0, 1, 0, 1, 0, 1, 1, 1, 0, 0, 1, 0, 1, 0, 1,
0, 1, 0, 0, 1, 1, 1, 1, 1, 1, 1, 0, 0, 0, 1, 0, 1, 1, 1, 0, 1, 1, 0, 1,
0, 1, 1, 1, 1, 0, 0, 0, 0, 0, 0, 0, 1]

flip all coins of 1st pile
1st piles coins after a flip: [1, 0, 0, 1, 1, 1, 0, 0, 1, 1, 1, 1,
1, 0, 0, 0, 0, 1, 1, 0, 1, 1, 1, 1, 1, 1, 1, 1, 1, 1, 0, 1, 0, 0, 0, 1,
0, 0, 1, 1, 0, 1, 1, 1, 0, 1, 0]

Number of coins with head in 1st pile: 29
Number of coins with head in 2nd pile: 29

Run again and output:
Randomly Generated Coins
[0, 1, 0, 1, 1, 1, 0, 0, 0, 0, 0, 1, 1, 1, 0, 0, 0, 1, 0, 0, 0, 1, 0,
0, 0, 0, 1, 0, 1, 0, 0, 1, 0, 1, 1, 0, 1, 0, 0, 0, 0, 1, 0, 0, 1, 0, 1,
0, 1, 1, 0, 1, 1, 1, 0, 1, 1, 0, 1, 1, 0, 1, 1, 0, 1, 1, 1, 1, 1, 0, 1,
1, 1, 1, 0, 0, 0, 0, 1, 1, 1, 1, 1, 0, 1, 0, 0, 0, 1, 1, 0, 0, 1, 1, 0,
0, 0, 1, 0, 1]

In single pile of 100 coins: 50 are Heads and 50 are Tails

Solution for splitting the coins into two piles
Size of 1st piles coins: 50
1st piles coins: [0, 1, 0, 1, 1, 1, 0, 0, 0, 0, 0, 1, 1, 1, 0, 0, 0, 1, 0, 0, 0, 1, 0, 0, 0, 0, 1, 0, 1, 0, 0, 1, 0, 1, 1, 0, 1, 0, 0, 0, 0, 1, 0, 0, 1, 0, 1, 0, 1, 1]
Size of 2nd piles coins: 50
2nd piles coins: [0, 1, 1, 1, 0, 1, 1, 0, 1, 1, 0, 1, 1, 0, 1, 1, 1, 1, 1, 0, 1, 1, 1, 1, 0, 0, 0, 0, 1, 1, 1, 1, 1, 0, 1, 0, 0, 0, 1, 1, 0, 0, 1, 1, 0, 0, 0, 1, 0, 1]
flip all coins of 1st pile
1st piles coins after a flip: [1, 0, 1, 0, 0, 0, 1, 1, 1, 1, 1, 0, 0, 0, 1, 1, 1, 0, 1, 1, 1, 0, 1, 1, 1, 1, 0, 1, 0, 1, 1, 0, 1, 0, 0, 1, 0, 1, 1, 1, 1, 0, 1, 1, 0, 1, 0, 1, 0, 0]
Number of coins with head in 1st pile: 30
Number of coins with head in 2nd pile: 30

8 N BAGS SOLUTION

There is only 1 bag with forgeries, so take 1 coin from the first bag, 2 coins from the second bag . . . N coins from the Nth bag and simply weigh the picked coins together.

If there were no forgeries, you know that the total weight should be $(1+2+...+n) = n*(n+1)/2$ grams.

So, the number difference between them will give the bag number of fake coins.

```python
# Finding Bag No filled with fake coins

from random import randint


# N Number of bags
N = 200
print('Total number of bags:', N)

# r Any random number between 1 & N
r = randint(1, N)
print('random bag number where to put
fake coins:', r)

coinArr = []
sumCoin = 0.0
```

```
#Putting 1 g coins in each bag except r
in which putting 1.1g fake coins
for x in range(1,N+1):
    if x == r :
        coinArr.append(1.1)
    else:
        coinArr.append(1)

print('Coin Bags:', coinArr)

#Finding fake coin bags
#Taking k numbers of coin from k bags &
weighing them
for k in range(len(coinArr)):
    sumCoin += (coinArr[k]) * (k+1)

print('Weight with fake coins:',
sumCoin)


#Wanted weight if no coins are fake
actualSumCoin = N * (N+1) / 2;

#Difference between sumCoin and
actualSumCoin
diff = sumCoin - actualSumCoin

#round function for correcting floating
point difference in Python
fakeBagNo = round(diff,4)*10

print('Bag No. with fake coins:',
round(fakeBagNo))
```

Total number of bags: 200
random bag number where to put fake coins: 195
Coin Bags: [1, 1, 1, 1, 1, 1, 1, 1, 1, 1, 1, 1, 1, 1, 1, 1, 1, 1,
1, 1, 1, 1, 1, 1, 1, 1, 1, 1, 1, 1, 1, 1, 1, 1, 1, 1, 1, 1, 1, 1, 1,
1, 1, 1, 1, 1, 1, 1, 1, 1, 1, 1, 1, 1, 1, 1, 1, 1, 1, 1, 1, 1, 1, 1,
1, 1, 1, 1, 1, 1, 1, 1, 1, 1, 1, 1, 1, 1, 1, 1, 1, 1, 1, 1, 1, 1, 1,
1, 1, 1, 1, 1, 1, 1, 1, 1, 1, 1, 1, 1, 1, 1, 1, 1, 1, 1, 1, 1, 1, 1,
1, 1, 1, 1, 1, 1, 1, 1, 1, 1, 1, 1, 1, 1, 1, 1, 1, 1, 1, 1, 1, 1, 1,
1, 1, 1, 1, 1, 1, 1, 1, 1, 1, 1, 1, 1, 1, 1, 1, 1, 1, 1, 1, 1, 1, 1,
1, 1, 1, 1, 1, 1, 1, 1, 1, 1, 1, 1, 1, 1, 1, 1, 1, 1, 1, 1, 1, 1, 1,
1, 1, 1, 1, 1, 1, 1, 1, 1.1, 1, 1, 1, 1, 1]
Weight with fake coins: 20119.5
Bag No. with fake coins: 195

Run again and output:
Total number of bags: 200
random bag number where to put fake coins: 12
Coin Bags: [1, 1, 1, 1, 1, 1, 1, 1, 1, 1, 1, 1.1, 1, 1, 1, 1, 1,
1, 1, 1, 1, 1, 1, 1, 1, 1, 1, 1, 1, 1, 1, 1, 1, 1, 1, 1, 1, 1, 1, 1,
1, 1, 1, 1, 1, 1, 1, 1, 1, 1, 1, 1, 1, 1, 1, 1, 1, 1, 1, 1, 1, 1, 1,
1, 1, 1, 1, 1, 1, 1, 1, 1, 1, 1, 1, 1, 1, 1, 1, 1, 1, 1, 1, 1, 1, 1,
1, 1, 1, 1, 1, 1, 1, 1, 1, 1, 1, 1, 1, 1, 1, 1, 1, 1, 1, 1, 1, 1, 1,
1, 1, 1, 1, 1, 1, 1, 1, 1, 1, 1, 1, 1, 1, 1, 1, 1, 1, 1, 1, 1, 1, 1,
1, 1, 1, 1, 1, 1, 1, 1, 1, 1, 1, 1, 1, 1, 1, 1, 1, 1, 1, 1, 1, 1, 1,
1, 1, 1, 1, 1, 1, 1, 1, 1, 1, 1, 1, 1, 1, 1, 1, 1, 1, 1, 1, 1, 1, 1,
1, 1, 1, 1, 1, 1, 1, 1, 1, 1, 1, 1, 1, 1]
Weight with fake coins: 20101.2
Bag No. with fake coins: 12
>

9 RAIN IN THE CITY SOLUTION

You only require one of the friends to be telling the truth. The probability that at least one of them is telling the truth will be:

1 - (Probability that all of them Lied)

The probability that one of them lied is **1/N**
So, the probability that **all N lied is** $1/N * 1/N * 1/N \ldots * 1/N$ (N times multiplication of $1/N$) = **1/(N^N)**

So, now the probability that at least one of them told the truth is or there is a raining is: $1 - (1/(N^N))$

```
# Probability of Raining

import math

# N Number of friends
N = 3

# P Probability =1 - (Probability that
all of them Lied)
P = 1 - (1/pow(N,N))

print('Possibility of Raining',
P*100,'%')
```

If N=3 output:
Possibility of Raining 96.2962962962963 %

If N=2 then output:
Possibility of Raining 75.0 %

If N=5 then output:
Possibility of Raining 99.968 %

10 N PRISONERS & N BOXES SOLUTION

There is a strategy that provides a better survival probability than randomly opening the boxes.

To describe the strategy, not only the prisoners, but also the boxes are also numbered from 1 to N. The strategy is now as follows:

1.) Each prisoner first opens the box with his own number.
2.) If that box contains his number then he is successful.
3.) Otherwise, the box contains the number of another prisoner and he next opens the box with this number.
4.) The prisoner repeats steps 2 and 3 until he finds his own number or has opened N/2 drawers.

```
from random import randint

# Flling N Boxes randomly
def fillBoxes(N, NBox):

    r = randint(1, N)

    if r in NBox:
        fillBoxes(N, NBox)
    else:
        NBox.append(r)
        if(len(NBox) <N):
            fillBoxes(N, NBox)
```

```python
    return NBox

# Finding Own Number
def findingNumber(chosenOne, NBox,
checkBoxNo, count, N):
    if count >= N/2:
        if(NBox[checkBoxNo-1] ==
chosenOne):
            print('Number is found')
        else:
            print('Number is not
found')
        return
    elif(NBox[checkBoxNo-1] ==
chosenOne):
        print('Number is found')
        return 1
    else:
        print('At Step:', count+1,':
','checked box number:',
NBox[checkBoxNo-1])
        findingNumber(chosenOne, NBox,
NBox[checkBoxNo-1], count+1, N)


# N Number of Prisoners
N = 120

print('Total number of Prisoners', N)

# Fill N boxes randomly with numbers 1
to N
NBox = []
```

```
NBox = fillBoxes(N, NBox)
print('Arrangement of Boxes', NBox)


chosenOne = randint(1, N)
print('Prison No.', chosenOne,'is
sent')

print('At step: 1: checked box
number:', chosenOne)

findingNumber(chosenOne, NBox,
chosenOne, 1, N)
```

N=120 then Output:

Total number of Prisoners 120

Arrangement of Boxes [75, 33, 85, 83, 64, 108, 81, 100, 58, 15, 38, 92, 5, 36, 2, 13, 115, 49, 16, 63, 93, 99, 109, 67, 35, 29, 110, 30, 120, 86, 112, 9, 48, 21, 70, 111, 105, 89, 54, 8, 11, 84, 25, 101, 34, 44, 69, 72, 117, 4, 87, 102, 19, 103, 45, 39, 106, 119, 107, 95, 17, 91, 26, 51, 65, 73, 60, 1, 6, 82, 52, 94, 98, 97, 114, 12, 118, 10, 88, 79, 14, 24, 77, 61, 59, 96, 28, 57, 41, 7, 18, 78, 55, 74, 116, 90, 42, 3, 22, 40, 50, 31, 20, 113, 66, 76, 27, 62, 56, 80, 37, 68, 104, 53, 23, 47, 43, 71, 32, 46]

Prison No. 40 is sent

At step: 1: checked box number: 40

At Step: 2 : checked box number: 8

At Step: 3 : checked box number: 100

Number is found

N=100 then Output:

Total number of Prisoners 100

Arrangement of Boxes [63, 21, 19, 4, 94, 8, 3, 36, 11,

27, 80, 69, 2, 65, 24, 67, 92, 10, 82, 40, 39, 7, 87, 1, 14, 26,
78, 59, 43, 77, 51, 93, 31, 76, 32, 17, 41, 89, 29, 99, 73, 54,
52, 22, 6, 38, 98, 84, 66, 5, 70, 13, 46, 50, 68, 83, 15, 30, 74,
33, 18, 55, 62, 96, 56, 79, 16, 64, 75, 34, 42, 88, 85, 53, 48,
44, 95, 23, 20, 71, 12, 35, 28, 58, 9, 97, 57, 100, 47, 91, 49,
86, 90, 72, 25, 60, 81, 45, 61, 37]

Prison No. 3 is sent
At step: 1: checked box number: 3
At Step: 2 : checked box number: 19
At Step: 3 : checked box number: 82
At Step: 4 : checked box number: 35
At Step: 5 : checked box number: 32
At Step: 6 : checked box number: 93
At Step: 7 : checked box number: 90
At Step: 8 : checked box number: 91
At Step: 9 : checked box number: 49
At Step: 10 : checked box number: 66
At Step: 11 : checked box number: 79
At Step: 12 : checked box number: 20
At Step: 13 : checked box number: 40
At Step: 14 : checked box number: 99
At Step: 15 : checked box number: 61
At Step: 16 : checked box number: 18
At Step: 17 : checked box number: 10
At Step: 18 : checked box number: 27
At Step: 19 : checked box number: 78
At Step: 20 : checked box number: 23
At Step: 21 : checked box number: 87
At Step: 22 : checked box number: 57
At Step: 23 : checked box number: 15
At Step: 24 : checked box number: 24
At Step: 25 : checked box number: 1
At Step: 26 : checked box number: 63
At Step: 27 : checked box number: 62
At Step: 28 : checked box number: 55
At Step: 29 : checked box number: 68

At Step: 30 : checked box number: 64
At Step: 31 : checked box number: 96
At Step: 32 : checked box number: 60
At Step: 33 : checked box number: 33
At Step: 34 : checked box number: 31
At Step: 35 : checked box number: 51
At Step: 36 : checked box number: 70
At Step: 37 : checked box number: 34
At Step: 38 : checked box number: 76
At Step: 39 : checked box number: 44
At Step: 40 : checked box number: 22
At Step: 41 : checked box number: 7
Number is found

>

Again N=100 then Output:
Total number of Prisoners 100
Arrangement of Boxes [78, 30, 52, 67, 56, 49, 15, 82, 4,
34, 16, 77, 25, 43, 8, 38, 88, 97, 76, 87, 93, 41, 42, 94, 62,
79, 18, 36, 47, 84, 100, 73, 27, 90, 7, 5, 11, 32, 3, 46, 69, 63,
6, 99, 72, 22, 74, 35, 50, 85, 20, 55, 10, 29, 14, 60, 53, 89,
96, 54, 21, 26, 1, 33, 37, 64, 66, 92, 39, 40, 28, 91, 45, 9, 81,
70, 58, 65, 13, 83, 86, 71, 17, 23, 19, 2, 75, 51, 48, 12, 61,
68, 59, 57, 95, 44, 31, 98, 24, 80]
Prison No. 16 is sent
At step: 1: checked box number: 16
At Step: 2 : checked box number: 38
At Step: 3 : checked box number: 32
At Step: 4 : checked box number: 73
At Step: 5 : checked box number: 45
At Step: 6 : checked box number: 72
At Step: 7 : checked box number: 91
At Step: 8 : checked box number: 61
At Step: 9 : checked box number: 21
At Step: 10 : checked box number: 93
At Step: 11 : checked box number: 59

At Step: 12 : checked box number: 96
At Step: 13 : checked box number: 44
At Step: 14 : checked box number: 99
At Step: 15 : checked box number: 24
At Step: 16 : checked box number: 94
At Step: 17 : checked box number: 57
At Step: 18 : checked box number: 53
At Step: 19 : checked box number: 10
At Step: 20 : checked box number: 34
At Step: 21 : checked box number: 90
At Step: 22 : checked box number: 12
At Step: 23 : checked box number: 77
At Step: 24 : checked box number: 58
At Step: 25 : checked box number: 89
At Step: 26 : checked box number: 48
At Step: 27 : checked box number: 35
At Step: 28 : checked box number: 7
At Step: 29 : checked box number: 15
At Step: 30 : checked box number: 8
At Step: 31 : checked box number: 82
At Step: 32 : checked box number: 71
At Step: 33 : checked box number: 28
At Step: 34 : checked box number: 36
At Step: 35 : checked box number: 5
At Step: 36 : checked box number: 56
At Step: 37 : checked box number: 60
At Step: 38 : checked box number: 54
At Step: 39 : checked box number: 29
At Step: 40 : checked box number: 47
At Step: 41 : checked box number: 74
At Step: 42 : checked box number: 9
At Step: 43 : checked box number: 4
At Step: 44 : checked box number: 67
At Step: 45 : checked box number: 66
At Step: 46 : checked box number: 64
At Step: 47 : checked box number: 33

At Step: 48 : checked box number: 27
At Step: 49 : checked box number: 18
At Step: 50 : checked box number: 97
Number is not found
>

11 BALLS ON A PLANE SOLUTION

Generally, people will think the number of balls = (volume of plane) / (volume of a ball), but they forget about density index.

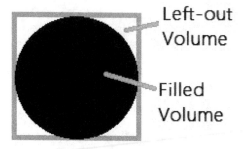

If there is a cube and we have to fit a sphere into it then,
Left-out volume = volume of cube – volume of sphere

$$= (2a)^3 - ((4/3) * pi * a^3)$$
$$= a^3 * (8 - ((4/3) * pi))$$
$$\sim 3.81\ a^3$$

Filled-out volume = volume of cube – Left-out volume
$$= 8a^3 - 3.81\ a^3$$
$$\sim 4.19a^3$$

Density index = Filled-out volume / Volume of Cube
$$= 4.19a^3 / 8a^3$$
$$\sim 0.53$$

But while arranging the balls optimally the density index increase, see the next image.

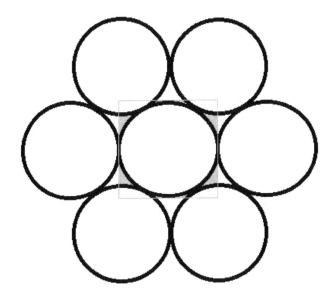

As you can see, the left-out volume is decreased.

A random packing of equal spheres generally has a density around 64%. So let's set our density index as 0.64

So our final equation is:

Number of Balls = $\dfrac{\text{Density Index} * \text{Volume of Plane}}{\text{Volume of Ball}}$

Let's take an example of a tennis ball with radius of 6.54 cm and a Boeing 747 plane with length of 71m and interior radius of 6m.

```
# Balls packing

import math

#r Radius of a ball in cm
r = 6.54

#R Interior radius of a plane in cm
R = 600
#L length of a plane in cm
L = 7100

#Volume of a ball
vBall = 4 * math.pi * (pow(r,3)) /3;


#Volume of a plane
vPlane = math.pi * L * (pow(R,2));

#p Packing Density
p = 0.64

#N Number of Balls
N = math.ceil(p*vPlane/vBall)

print('Possible number of balls to fit
into a plane:', N)
```

Output:
Possible number of balls to fit into a plane: 4386003

Now, given that golf ball radius is 4.267 cm while Boeing 747 is 70.66 meters long and 7.5 meters interior radius. How many golf balls can fit inside a Boeing 747?
You have to set
r = 4.267
R = 750
L = 7066
And run the program and get an output.

Possible number of balls to fit into a plane: 24556670

12 4 N SOLUTION

$N + [(N/N).N]$
$= N + [1.N]$ ⟵ Decimcal Point
$= N+1.N$

Let's take an example if N=6 then
6 + [(6/6).6] = 6 + [1.6] = 6+1.6 = 7.6

```
from random import randint

# generate random number between 1-999,
both inclusive
input = randint(1, 999)
print('input:',input)

#output
output =
str(round(input+(input/input))) + '.' +
str(input)
print('output:',output)
```

Let's run the program.
input: 125
output: 126.125

Run again
input: 19
output: 20.19

13 N-DISTANCES SOLUTION

If total length of the roads connecting those cities is the minimum then it's cost too.

At the first, most people think about the diagonals of a square, but it is not an optimal solution. The optimal solution is the Steiner tree as shown next.

Minimum $L{\approx}2.732$

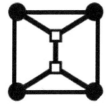 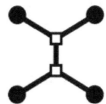

Other Options:
$L_\sqcap=3, L_\times{\approx}2.828$

As shown in given image if we connect the cities (N distances away) by the diagonals of a square then,
Length of a connecting road = 2.828*N

But in the case of Steiner tree this cost is reduced to 2.732*N.

```
from random import randint

# generate random number between 1-99,
both inclusive
input = randint(1, 99)
print('Distance between any two
adjacent corner cities:',input)
print('Minimum cost:',
round(input*2.732,2))
```

Let's run the program.

Distance between any two adjacent corner cities: 20
Minimum cost: 54.64

Run again
Distance between any two adjacent corner cities: 12
Minimum cost: 32.78

Run again
Distance between any two adjacent corner cities: 16
Minimum cost: 43.71

14 THE PENTAGON SOLUTION

Star mesh topology is one of the solutions but it is not an optimal one. This is again the Steiner tree problem with five points.

In case of the Star mesh topology, for a pentagon with side length of N meters,
Total construction cost = 4.253 * N * R

In case of the Steiner tree with five corner points, for a pentagon with side length of N meters,
Total minimum construction cost = 3.891 * N * R

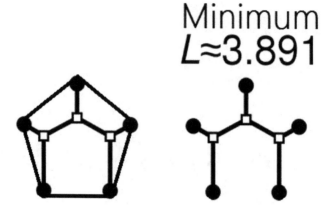

Minimum
$L \approx 3.891$

Other Options:
$L_\curvearrowright = 4, L_* \approx 4.253$

```
from random import randint

# generate random number between 1-50,
both inclusive
input = randint(1, 50)
print('Distance between any two
adjacent corners of Pentagon
building:',input, 'meters')
print('Minimum cost:',
round(input*3.891,2),'* R')
```

Let's run the program.
Distance between any two adjacent corners of Pentagon
building: 11 meters
Minimum cost: 42.8 * R

Run again
Distance between any two adjacent corners of Pentagon
building: 10 meters
Minimum cost: 38.91 * R

15 N COLORS CHAMELEONS SOLUTION

$(C_1, C_2, ...$ and $C_N)$ - Configuration is reducible to a single color configuration if and only if at least 2 of the quantities $C_1, C_2, ...$ and C_N have the same remainder of division by N.

Here, N = Number of colors &

$C_1, C_2, ..., C_N$ = Initial quantity of the chameleons of respective color

```
#N COLORS CHAMELEONS

from random import randint

#n color type between 3-10, both
inclusive
n = randint(3, 10)
print('Total', n, 'colors of
chameleons')

# Number of chameleons by colors
```

```
noChameByCol = []

# Setting initial amounts of the
chameleons of each color
for x in range(n):
    #add random numbers between 1-50
    noChameByCol.append(randint(1, 30))


print('Initial amounts of the
chameleons of each color:',

noChameByCol)

quotientArr = []

# Calculation quotient of mod n and
checking if any two quantities have the
same remainder of division by N
count = 0
for x in range(len(noChameByCol)):
    q, r = divmod(noChameByCol[x], n)
    if(r in quotientArr):
        count = 1
        break
    else:
        quotientArr.append(r)

if(count == 1):
    print('Reducible to single color
chameleons')
else:
```

```
    print('Can not reducible to single
color chameleons')
```

Let's run the program.

Total 3 colors of chameleons
Initial amounts of the chameleons of each color: [28, 12, 22]
Reducible to single color chameleons
Total 3 colors of chameleons
Initial amounts of the chameleons of each color: [22, 9, 14]
Can not reducible to single color chameleons
Total 5 colors of chameleons
Initial amounts of the chameleons of each color: [25, 7, 21, 4, 20]
Reducible to single color chameleons

Total 6 colors of chameleons
Initial amounts of the chameleons of each color: [15, 29, 2, 1, 4, 18]
Can not reducible to single color chameleons

Total 4 colors of chameleons
Initial amounts of the chameleons of each color: [21, 20, 25, 29]
Reducible to single color chameleons

Brain Teasers with Coding for Data Scientist

ABOUT AUTHOR

"I'm a computer engineer and a software consultant. I'm extremely fond of anything that is related to mathematics, computer science and creative ideas. You can contact me at viragbook@gmail.com"

- VIRAG R. SHAH

www.ingramcontent.com/pod-product-compliance
Lightning Source LLC
La Vergne TN
LVHW051614050326
832903LV00033B/4486